ELIJAH THE PROPHET

VOLUME 1

TJ WALTON
ILLUSTRATOR HALEY WALTON

XULON PRESS

Xulon Press
2301 Lucien Way #415
Maitland, FL 32751
407.339.4217
www.xulonpress.com

© 2020 by TJ Walton
Illustrator Haley Walton

Unless otherwise indicated, Scripture quotations taken from the King James Version (KJV)–*public domain.*

Paperback ISBN-13: 978-1-6312-9625-3
Hard Cover ISBN-13: 978-1-6312-9626-0

CHAPTER 1

LET ME TELL YOU
ABOUT ELIJAH.

ELIJAH IS A LITTLE BOY WHO IS
KIND AND SWEET.

HE CAME INTO THE WORLD,
FIRST AS A BABY.

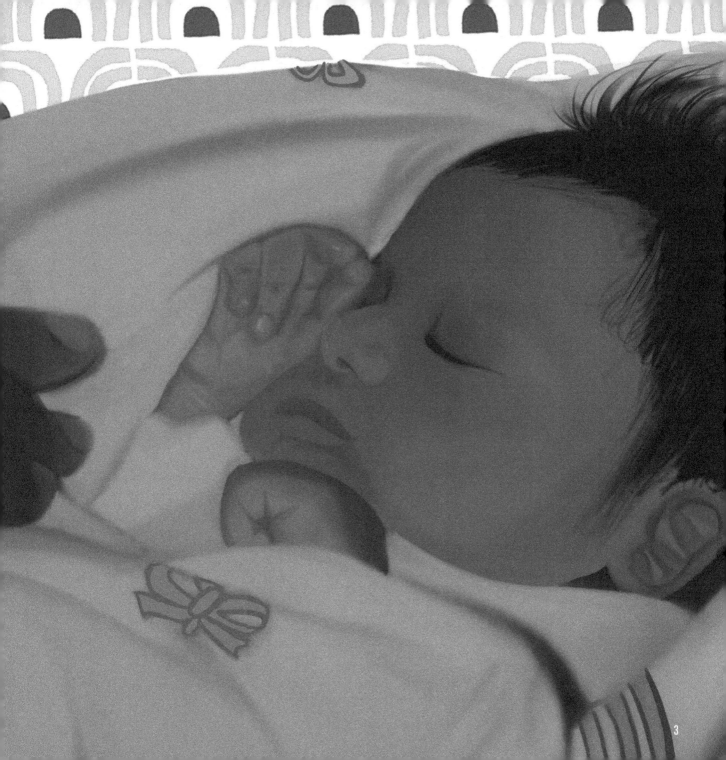

HE WAS A BIG BABY BOY.

HE WEIGHED 9.7 POUNDS AND WAS VERY LONG.

HE WAS 22 AND A HALF INCHES LONG.

ELIJAH WAS A SMART LITTLE BABY.

HE WAS QUIET BUT ALWAYS THINKING.

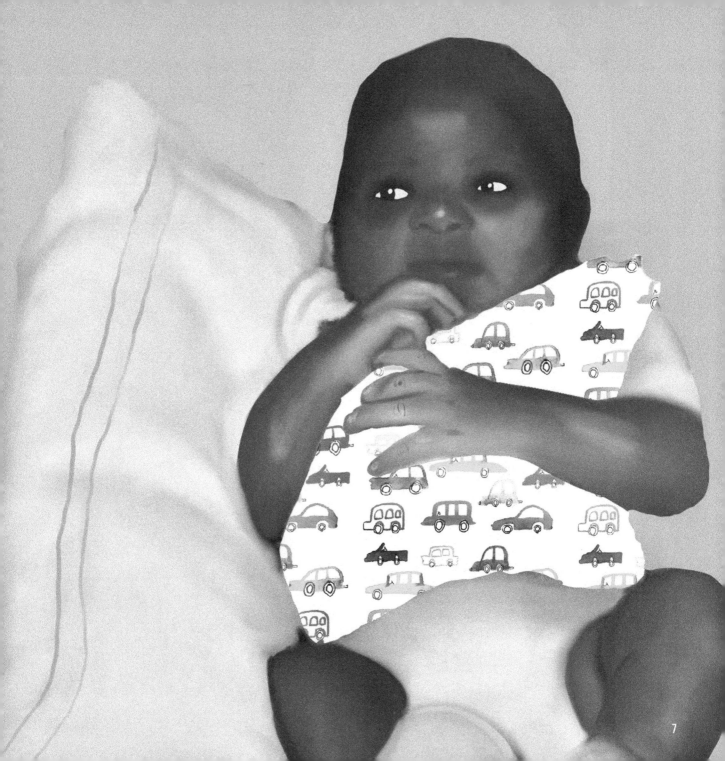

HE HAD BIG BEAUTIFUL DARK BROWN EYES AND FAT ROUND CHEEKS.

ELIJAH SITS IN HIS MOTHER ARMS AND JUST STARES WITH HIS BIG DARK BROWN EYES.

ELIJAH'S MOTHER WONDERS WHAT HE IS THINKING.

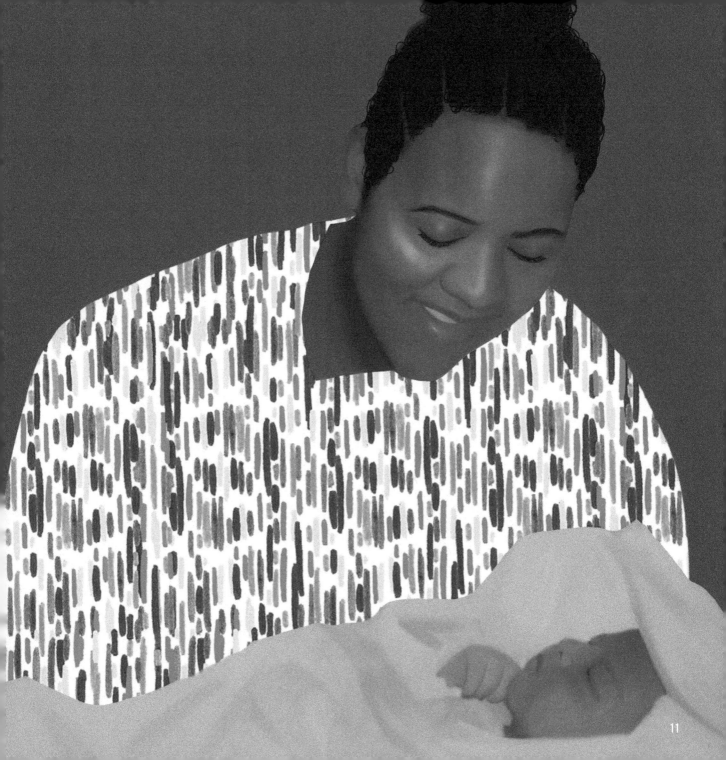

AS ELIJAH STARTED LIFE, HE BEGAN TO LEARN ABOUT THE BIG WORLD ALL AROUND HIM.

THOSE BIG DARK BROWN EYES WERE LOOKING EVERYWHERE.

ALTHOUGH HE WAS STILL A BABY, SOON HE WOULD LEARN TO TALK.

A BABY WONDER, A BABY BOY.
ELIJAH, THE PROPHET.

ELIJAH IS A MIRACLE BABY. WHEN HE WAS BORN THE DOCTOR RUSHED TO HELP HIM COME TO LIFE. HIS MOTHER'S CHORD WAS WRAPPED TWICE AROUND HIS NECK.

WOW! THE DOCTOR HAD TO UNTIE THE CHORDS SO THAT BABY ELIJAH COULD LIVE! GOD HAD A PLAN AND PURPOSE FOR ELIJAH'S LIFE. THANK GOD BECAUSE ELIJAH THE PROPHET WAS BORN!!

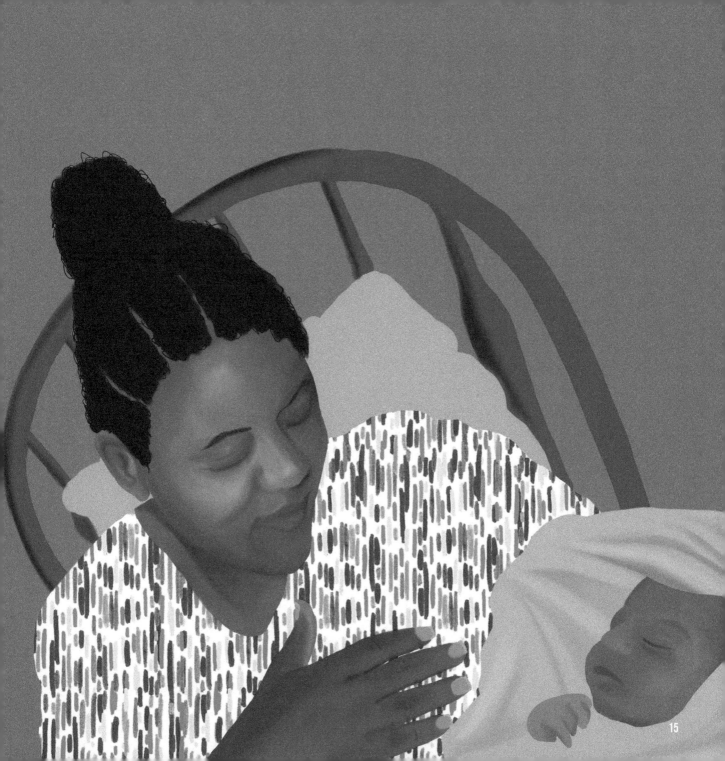

BABY ELIJAH BEGINS TO TALK

CHAPTER 2

AS ELIJAH STARTED LIFE, HE BEGAN TO LEARN ABOUT THE BIG WORLD ALL AROUND HIM. THOSE BIG DARK BROWN EYES WERE LOOKING EVERYWHERE. ALTHOUGH HE WAS STILL A BABY, SOON HE WOULD LEARN TO TALK.

HIS MOMMY AND DADDY PRAYED TO HIM EACH DAY AS A BABY. THEY WANTED HIM TO LEARN TO PRAY TOO.

ONCE HE STARTED TO TALK HIS FIRST WORD WAS DA DA. DA DA MEANS DADDY.

SOMETIMES ELIJAH'S MOMMY AND DADDY WOULD SAY DA DA TO ELIJAH AND HE WOULD SAY IT TOO.

HIS PARENTS WOULD LAUGH AND BABY ELIJAH WOULD LAUGH TOO.

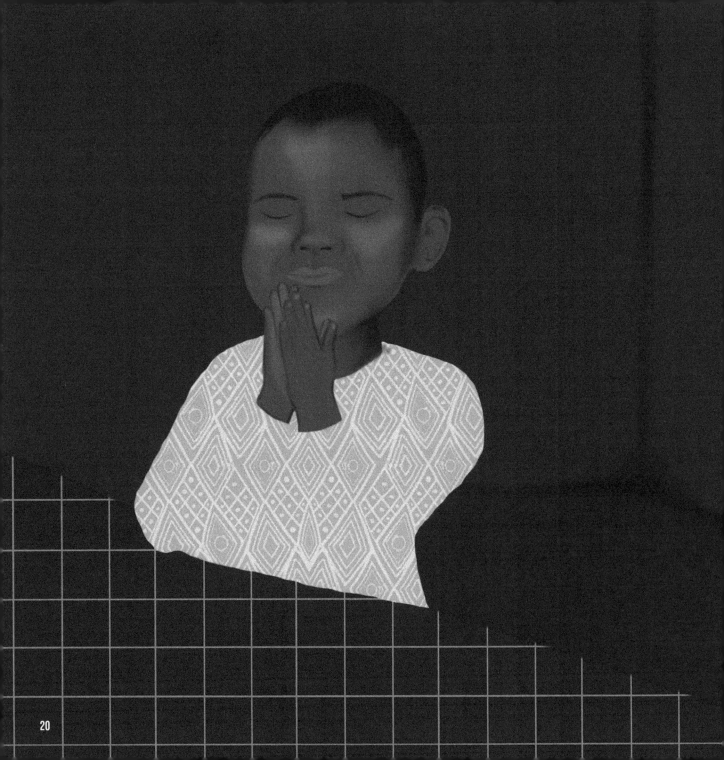

SOON, ELIJAH LEARNED TO PRAY.

HE LOVED TO PRAY AT MEAL TIME.

HE COULD NOT SAY MUCH BUT HE
COULD SAY AMEN.

BABY ELIJAH WAS A SPECIAL BABY.

HE WAS A PROPHET.

HE WAS BORN WITH A SPECIAL TOUCH ON HIS LIFE.

HIS PURPOSE WAS TO LOVE THE LORD AND GROW UP TO TELL OTHERS ABOUT GOD AND HOW HE CAME INTO THE WORLD.

HIS FAMILY LOVED HIM VERY MUCH.

TRUDY JENISE WALTON

TJ IS A POET, WRITER AND RETIRED EDUCATOR WHO SPENT HER CAREER ADVOCATING STUDENT SUCCESS AND THE AUTHOR OF "ELIJAH THE PROPHET". HER ENTHUSIASM TO WRITE CHILDREN BOOKS COMES FROM HER PERSONAL EXPERIENCE OF BEING A MOM. THIS BOOK IS INSPIRED BY THE EXPERIENCE OF MOTHERHOOD. ELIJAH THE PROPHET IS ONE OF HER WORKS TOWARDS MANIFESTING THE GOALS OF HER VISION OF WRITING CHILDREN'S BOOKS.

BORN IN MEMPHIS, TENNESSEE AND REARED IN LORAIN, OHIO, AS A CHILD AND TEENAGER, SHE WAS CONSUMED WITH WRITING POETRY AND ASPIRED TO BE A JOURNALIST. TJ WAS INTERESTED IN BROADCAST JOURNALISM. AFTER COMPLETING SEVERAL COLLEGE DEGREES AND SERVING AS A COLLEGE ADMINISTRATOR, SHE IS ABLE TO DEDICATE TIME TO HER PASSION OF WRITING.

SHE LOVES FAMILY AND ENJOYS HELPING OTHERS. HER LIFE WORK HAS BEEN DEDICATED TO THE SERVITUDE OF HELPING STUDENTS ACHIEVE THEIR GOALS, ASPIRATIONS AND DREAMS. SHE IS CURRENTLY WRITING A SECOND VOLUME OF ELIJAH THE PROPHET BOOK.

IN HER LEISURE TIME SHE ENJOYS ATTENDING SPORTS EVENTS WITH HER SON AND TRAVELING, READING AND WRITING.

CPSIA information can be obtained
at www.ICGtesting.com
Printed in the USA
LVHW071609080720
660121LV00013B/1542